975.3   C-3

5895

Jones, Lois Perry
The first book of the White
House

DATE DUE			
FEB 16 '68			
3-P			
P-3			
5-B			
FEB 1971			
JAN 25			

GAYLORD M-2   PRINTED IN U.S.A.

The FIRST BOOK of THE WHITE HOUSE

I Pray Heaven to Bestow

The Best of Blessings on

THIS HOUSE

and on All that shall hereafter

Inhabit it. May none but Honest

and Wise Men ever rule

under This Roof !

John Adams
Nov. 2, 1800

The FIRST BOOK of

THE WHITE HOUSE

HOME — OFFICE — MUSEUM

by Lois Perry Jones

Illustrated by Leonard Everett Fisher

FRANKLIN WATTS , INC.
575 Lexington Ave. New York, N.Y. 10022

For security reasons, diagrams of cer-
tain parts of the White House, including the living quarters and the
offices, are not available.

3   4   5
Copyright © 1965 by Franklin Watts, Inc.
Library of Congress Catalog Card Number: 65-11383
Printed in the United States of America by
Polygraphic Company of America

Contents

The FIRST BOOK of THE WHITE HOUSE

We acknowledge with thanks the assistance of Mr. James R. Ketchum, Curator of the White House, in reviewing both the manuscript and the illustrations of this book.

What Is the White House?

"I PRAY HEAVEN to bestow the best of Blessings on this House and all that shall hereafter inhabit it. May none but honest and wise Men ever rule under this roof."

Those are the words of John Adams, second President of the United States. He was writing about one of the most famous and important buildings in the world — the White House at 1600 Pennsylvania Avenue, Washington, D. C.

What is the White House? It is actually three buildings in one. It is a mansion, the home of the President of the United States. The President and his family live in the White House and entertain their personal friends there. It is an office building, containing the only office of the President of the United States. From there, the President, with the help of his staff, directs the affairs of one of the most powerful nations on earth. It is also the ceremonial headquarters of our country. Each year it is visited by great numbers of tourists (nearly two million in 1964), and in it the President entertains great and important people from every part of the United States, and from all over the world.

The White House has been the home of the President, the office of the President, and the ceremonial headquarters of our country ever since the building was opened in 1800. All but one of our Presidents have lived and worked there. The man who never lived in the President's House, as it was then called, was George Washington. However, he laid the cornerstone and supervised the building of the mansion.

1

When the White House was new, it was surrounded by the President's Park, just as it is today. The land on which it stands cost $1,000 and the House itself $400,000. It is built of Virginia sandstone, which is actually buff in color rather than white. It was then, and is now, 168 feet long and 85 feet wide. When the House was first used, only six of its rooms were finished, and it had no bathrooms and no closets. The ground floor was used for storage space. Water was carried into the White House from a well.

Since that time, the population of the United States has increased from 5 million to nearly 200 million persons. The country has grown from a small republic of thirteen states to a large and powerful nation with fifty states. The White House has changed as the country has changed, and it has grown in size and importance as the country has grown.

Below is the White House as it was originally built, and, right, the White House as it is today.

As it was designed by architect James Hoban in 1792, it was only three stories high. Now it has six stories: three from the first floor up, and three from the ground floor down. Attached to the East side and the West side of the White House are large three-story wings. The Ground Floor and the First Floor are the ceremonial headquarters of the White House. The Second Floor is where the President lives. The Third Floor has guest bedrooms, servants' quarters, and a sky-lighted recreation room. The two floors below the Ground Floor contain nearly fifty utility and storage rooms. The West Wing holds the President's Office and the offices of his assistants. The East Wing includes offices for the Secret Service, the White House police, military aides, and the First Lady's secretaries.

Twenty-three different kinds of marble and stone were used to build the White House. When it was renovated during 1949 to 1952, eight hundred tons of steel and sixty tons of cement were needed to build the inside. It has half a million feet of electrical wiring and more than two thousand electric plugs and switches.

Inside the White House are 132 rooms, 69 closets, 3 elevators, 146 windows, 712 doors, and 29 fireplaces. Included in the House and its wings are a medical clinic, a dentist's room, a barber room, a swimming pool, and a motion-picture theater.

Over 500 people regularly work in and around the White House. About 70 people take care of the White House proper and the President's Park. About 270 persons work in the White House Office. Secret Service men and 170 White House policemen guard the President, his family, and the White House Office.

Many books have been written which tell of the long and colorful history of the White House. Others describe in great detail the interesting decorations inside the building. This book will tell you about the White House as it is today, and the way in which it functions in three separate ways.

The President's Home

WHEN THE WHITE HOUSE was first built, the United States was small and the President's duties were light. No one thought that it would be difficult to use the White House as a ceremonial mansion and an office as well as a home. It was expected that the President would use the whole House as a home, reserving a room or two for his office, and, when needed, using the First Floor rooms to entertain his personal and official guests.

So the kitchen was put on the Ground Floor, the family dining room on the First Floor, and the President's Office and family bedrooms on the Second Floor.

The plan would have worked very well if the country had stayed small. However, before too many years had passed, the early Presidents and their families found that it was difficult to lead a normal family life in the White House. They didn't have any privacy. Visitors and job seekers wandered in and out of the public rooms on the First Floor, and tramped up and down the staircase to the President's Office on the Second Floor.

So, after a hundred years, the offices of the President were moved from the Second Floor into the West Wing, which was built in 1902.

Today, the President's living quarters are located on the Second Floor. Here are the family's sitting rooms, bedrooms, a dining room, and a kitchen. Here the President can lead as private a life as is possible in a house filled with many servants. Here the President and his family can entertain their personal friends.

7

Because the Second Floor wasn't planned to provide complete living quarters for the President and his family, and because Presidential families have varied greatly in size and taste, most of the rooms on the Second Floor have been used in several different ways.

The hall which runs down the center of the building from the East end of the House to the West end is divided into three sitting rooms. On the East end is the Guests' Sitting Room, and on the West end is the Family Sitting Room. The central portion of the hall is known as the Gallery Sitting Room.

On the South side of the Family Sitting Room, which is comfortably furnished with sofas, chairs, coffee tables, and a desk, are two doors leading to bedrooms. On the North side are doors leading to the Dining Room and the kitchen, which were installed during John F. Kennedy's years in office. Three other bedrooms and a drawing room open off the Gallery Sitting Room.

In these rooms, and in the recreation room and sky parlor on the Third Floor, the President and his family can relax and enjoy a personal life. President Roosevelt's wife served tea in the Family Sitting Room, and President and Mrs. Eisenhower often watched television here while they ate dinner.

In the Dining Room, a shirt-sleeved President Kennedy occasionally served dinner to his guests when Mrs. Kennedy was away. In President Truman's time, his daughter Margaret kept her piano there. The Third Floor recreation room housed Caroline Kennedy's schoolroom before Lynda and Luci Johnson used it for their activities.

The rooms on the West end of the Second Floor are more personal and private than the rooms on the East end. This end of the floor once contained public offices, waiting rooms, and conference rooms.

One of the most famous of these rooms is the Lincoln Bedroom, which was once Lincoln's Cabinet Room and is now used as a guest room for male visitors. It was in this room that President Lincoln signed the Emancipation Proclamation, which freed the slaves, on January 1, 1863. In the room is a huge bed with a high carved headboard. It was purchased during Lincoln's administration.

8

The Rose Guest Room, on the North side of the House directly across from the Lincoln Bedroom, is used as a guest room for distinguished lady visitors. It is also called the Queen's Bedroom because five reigning queens have stayed there. They included Queen Elizabeth II of Great Britain and, many years ago, Queen Elizabeth's

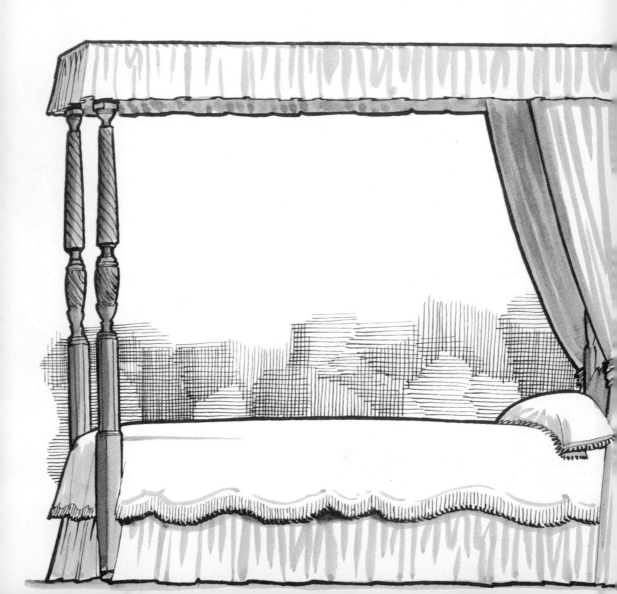

mother. Decorated in pink, rose, and white, the room contains a bed which is said to have belonged to Andrew Jackson, the seventh President of the United States.

Next to the Lincoln Bedroom and directly across the hall from the staircase, on the South side of the House, is the Treaty Room. This

room served as the President's Cabinet Room from just after the Civil War until 1902, when it became a sitting room. Now it is a meeting room for the President. Furnished in a rich and heavy Victorian manner, the room gets its name from the fact that the treaty which ended the Spanish-American War was signed there.

The Gallery Sitting Room, which is a waiting and reception room for dignitaries and Presidential guests, leads into the Yellow Oval Drawing Room. This room, in the center of the South side on the Second Floor, is one of three oval rooms in the White House. It is directly above the Blue Room on the First Floor, and the Diplomatic Reception Room on the Ground Floor. Originally designed to be a sitting room, it has been used as an office, a library, and a private study. Now the room is elegantly decorated in yellow and white, and furnished with delicate French furniture.

This is a diagram of these famous rooms on the Second Floor.

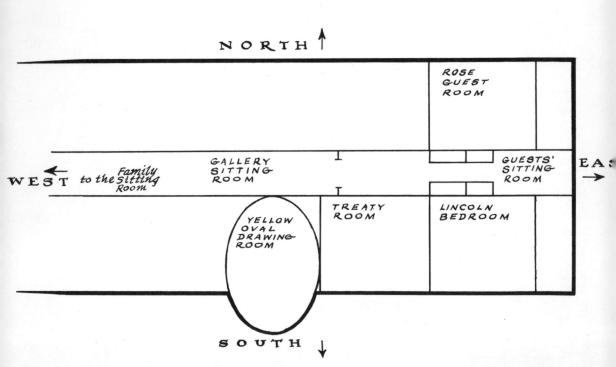

Whether or not the President has guests visiting him, he and his family are never really alone in the White House. Besides the Secret Service men who are constantly nearby, about seventy persons are needed to keep the White House in working order.

The domestic and maintenance staff is headed by the Chief Usher. He must make sure that the House and the grounds are always in perfect order. In a single day, he may see to it that a hundred chairs are brought up from the storerooms for a large social gathering; direct some needed repair work; arrange to have some visiting dignitaries escorted to the President's Office; and see that the gardeners do some necessary work in the Rose Garden, just outside the President's Office.

In 1963, the Chief Usher's staff included a chief butler and a head chef, two housekeepers, six cooks, four waiters, a valet, five doormen, five housemen, a laundress, a pantry woman, and eight maids. Others on the staff included eight engineers, four carpenters, four electricians, three plumbers, two storekeepers, a painter, ten laborers, and eleven gardeners.

Each of our Presidents has had his own personal likes and dislikes. And each of our First Ladies has so ordered life at the White House that it has reflected both the President's tastes and her own personality.

Abigail Adams, the first First Lady to live in the White House, was there only four months before a new President took office. However, she accomplished a great deal in those four months. When she moved in, only six rooms could be used. She didn't have enough wood for the thirteen fireplaces, and she didn't have enough lamps. But scarcely two months later, she and President Adams held a formal New Year's Day reception in the Oval Drawing Room on the Second Floor.

Thomas Jefferson was very interested in making the White House a comfortable place in which the President could live and work. He had terraces built east and west of the House. Frame buildings for offices, stables, and storage sheds were built on the terraces. He

brought his own furniture with him from his home at Monticello in Virginia. He gave brilliant dinner parties for which his French cook prepared foods then unknown in the United States, such as macaroni and ice cream.

Dolley Madison, wife of our fourth President, was cheerful and friendly. She, too, loved to entertain, and she gave magnificent parties. During her husband's terms in office, the White House was burned by the British in the War of 1812. After the fire, only its blackened sandstone walls stood. Mrs. Madison was able to save very few belongings from the fire. However, she did save the painting of George Washington which had been in the White House since 1800, and which today hangs in the East Room.

The White House was rebuilt by 1818 at a cost of $500,000. James Monroe and his family decorated the House with furniture that they bought in France, and social life began again. President Monroe held Wednesday night receptions to which any citizen was invited to come. Many different kinds of people came to these receptions. Some guests had powdered hair; others had hair that was frizzled and uncombed. Some guests wore shoes, others boots and spurs. Once the guests included a party of Indian chiefs, dressed in beads and painted red and yellow.

John Quincy Adams led a quiet life in the White House. He loved to watch the sunrise from his window, swim in the nearby Potomac River, and walk in his garden. He usually dined quietly, and went to bed around 10 P.M. When the President did entertain, the parties were very formal and exclusive.

After Andrew Jackson was inaugurated in 1829, social life at the White House changed again. First the President completed the decorations for the East Room. He bought chandeliers, gilded tables topped with Indian marble, and drapes of blue and yellow. Guests who attended his luxurious dinners found the White House glowing with lights of hundreds of wax candles and wood fires. But the President liked to spend evenings quietly, too. Surrounded by his family, he would sit upstairs, wearing a long loose coat and smoking a long pipe with a red clay bowl.

President Van Buren decided that the White House needed a good housecleaning, and he was accused of trying to turn it into a palace.

John Tyler was a widower and married for the second time after he became President. His wife, who was twenty-three years old when she became First Lady, tried to establish a very regal social life in the White House. However, Congress refused to spend any money on the mansion. It grew so dingy that it became known as the "Public Shabby House."

For the next few years, social life in the White House seemed very sedate. When James Buchanan, a wealthy bachelor, took office in 1857, the White House once more became the center of a brilliant social life. Serving as hostess was the President's blond and blue-eyed niece, Harriet Lane. Among the guests she entertained were the first Japanese envoys ever to visit the United States, and the Prince of Wales. When the Prince visited the White House, there were so many guests that the President had to sleep in the hall.

President Lincoln was too concerned with the Civil War to care very much about his social life, but during the first winter of the War, his wife entertained a great deal. President Lincoln was not a rich man. His wife, however, loved to spend money, which did not make the President very happy. Mrs. Lincoln is supposed to have bought three hundred pairs of gloves in four months.

In 1865, President Andrew Johnson brought his large family from Tennessee to live in the White House. When they arrived, the House was in a terrible condition. Soldiers had slept in the East Room during the Civil War. The furniture was full of bugs and stained with tobacco juice. The curtains were worn out and the rugs threadbare. President Johnson's daughter had the place cleaned from top to bottom, and ordered linen slipcovers for the furniture.

When Ulysses S. Grant, a famous general, entered the White House in 1869, it was renovated in the latest style. The old furniture was replaced by new furniture of ebony and gold. The East Room was decorated with gilded wallpaper. Washington society was delighted to be entertained by the easygoing, cigar-smoking General. They

17

flocked to the White House where dinners of twenty-five to thirty courses were served. One of the social highlights at the White House was the wedding of the President's daughter. The bridal couple stood under a wedding bell made of roses and baby's breath, and the banquet menus were printed on white satin.

President Chester Arthur liked to hold small dinner parties in the private dining room on the First Floor. He had it decorated with gold wallpaper, rose-colored lamps, and heavy velvet drapes.

Grover Cleveland gave society another fashionable wedding to talk about. However, this one was unique. It was his own. President Cleveland is the only President to be married in the White House. On June 2, 1886, he married Frances Folsom, then twenty-three, in the Blue Room on the First Floor.

By the time Benjamin Harrison entered the White House in 1889, it was clear that more room was needed for the large Harrison family. There were so few bedrooms that if guests stayed overnight, Mrs. Harrison had a hard time finding a place for them to sleep. She couldn't persuade Congress to enlarge the White House, but she did have the hot-water heating system replaced with steam, and electric lights installed. She also started the collection of Presidential china which still continues and is displayed today in the China Room on the Ground Floor.

When Theodore Roosevelt came to the White House, there was no doubt that the building had to be enlarged. He and his wife had six very lively children. The White House was soon the scene of wrestling matches and roller-skating contests. The President was as lively as his children. He loved to go for a "stroll." Sometimes this meant a fifteen- to twenty-mile tramp through fields and woods. Once the President walked right into icy water up to his waist. "Come along," he called cheerfully to his companions. "We can get through all right."

In 1902, Congress appropriated $540,641 for the first major remodeling of the White House. The State Dining Room was enlarged and two new suites of bedrooms and baths were built. Then Congress allowed $65,196 for new offices for the President. When these

were completed, the President's family finally had the Second Floor to themselves. The name "The White House" became official; before that it was called "The Executive Mansion."

The man who followed President Roosevelt into office was so huge that he had to have a special bathtub built for him. It was large enough to hold four ordinary-sized men. William Howard Taft weighed over three hundred pounds and loved beefsteak for breakfast. His wife loved to entertain. Before Taft, policemen used to greet visitors at the door. Now the policemen were replaced by six doormen in livery.

There was little entertaining at the White House during Woodrow Wilson's terms in office, because these were World War I years. But that changed when the war was over and Warren G. Harding was inaugurated in 1921. Lights went on again all over the White House. President Harding was handsome and jovial. He worked only two or three hours a day and loved to play golf and poker with his friends.

Harding's death brought New Englander Calvin Coolidge into office. Silent and restrained, President Coolidge, nevertheless, had a good sense of humor. He made up nicknames for everybody and he loved practical jokes — such as pushing all the buttons on his desk at once. The White House was again renovated, and the Coolidges had to live in a private home for a while.

Herbert Hoover was very wealthy and set new records in entertaining. In four years, President and Mrs. Hoover dined alone only three times. Sometimes three or four thousand invitations were sent out for just one party.

There were many changes in the President's social life during Franklin Roosevelt's years in office. During World War II, Mrs. Roosevelt often invited wounded servicemen in to tea. Blackout curtains hung on the windows and troops manned machine guns on the roof. Despite being crippled by polio, President Roosevelt was energetic. In this way, Mrs. Roosevelt was like her husband. Sometimes she held a tea for about fifteen hundred guests in the afternoon, and invited another fifteen hundred for a reception that same evening.

An informal person, she liked to scramble eggs for Sunday supper guests. Once she served hot dogs at a picnic for the King and Queen of England.

During Harry Truman's first term in office, the White House, then almost one hundred and fifty years old, was found to be unsafe. The President and his family moved across the street to Blair House, the President's guest house, and the White House interior was completely replaced and enlarged. Two additional basement layers were dug. A new steel framework was erected inside the shell of the original outside walls. Although the entire building could have been rebuilt for less than it cost to replace the interior, it was felt that the old White House, so long a symbol of the nation, should be preserved. Even with the remodeling, the Trumans managed to do a lot of entertaining. In one three-month period, they had twenty-three overnight guests, and entertained seventy-eight hundred persons at official gatherings.

President Eisenhower liked to play golf and bridge, and he also like to broil steaks in the "sky parlor" on the Third Floor of the White House. He and his wife enjoyed spending weekends at their Gettysburg farm or at Camp David in the Catoctin Mountains in Maryland. The President could use any one of three cars to get there: a Cadillac, a bubble-top Lincoln that cost about $30,000, or a Chrysler Imperial with a sliding roof. The President also had two cabin cruisers to use, a four-engine Super-Constellation, two six-passenger Aero-Commanders, and a number of helicopters. Whenever he went anywhere by car, Secret Service agents followed him in a specially constructed Cadillac that cost about $65,000. In contrast to all this, President John Adams had one horse-drawn coach.

Shortly after President and Mrs. Kennedy moved into the White House in 1961, she said: "Everything we had came in little boxes, everything was confused. The painters were still working on the Second Floor, the windows wouldn't open, the fireplaces smoked. I wondered how we were ever going to live as a family in this enormous place." Once they were settled, however, the Kennedys usually invited personal friends in for informal dinners about twice a week.

When Mrs. Kennedy became First Lady, she determined that the decorations and interiors of the White House should reflect the whole history of the Presidency and American life. This idea had occurred to both Mrs. Coolidge and Mrs. Hoover, who started to restore the White House with beautiful pieces of furniture. Now Mrs. Kennedy, with a committee of experts to help her, successfully carried through an extensive plan to make the White House a showplace of the nation. This restoration has greatly interested the American public, and many people have sent gifts to furnish the White House.

When President and Mrs. Johnson moved into the White House, it was so lovely that few changes were made. However, the bedrooms which Caroline and John Kennedy used were redecorated for Lynda and Luci Johnson. Mrs. Johnson changed a dressing room into an office for herself, and hung paintings of Texas landscapes on the Second Floor. With two lively attractive daughters to serve as assistant hostesses, Mrs. Johnson filled the White House with a busy and informal social life.

The President's Office

THE WHITE HOUSE is the only office of the President of the United States. He does not have an office in the Capitol or anywhere else. Although the President conducts his business even when he travels or takes a vacation, generally people come to the White House to conduct business with him.

When the White House was first built, the President's Office consisted of one or two rooms on the First Floor and he had a staff of one or two clerks. Because the President had to pay the wages of the people who helped him, he frequently used members of his own family as secretaries. More than one President wrote out his letters himself.

Our country was sixty-five years old before Congress decided that it should pay the salaries of the President's staff. Then each year $2,500 was set aside for a secretary, $1,200 for a steward, and $900 for a messenger.

Even after the Civil War, the President's staff was small. President Grant had six clerks, and received only $13,800 annually from Congress for their wages and his other office expenses.

It wasn't until around 1890 that the White House office staff grew beyond ten persons, including the doorkeepers and the messengers. President McKinley had a staff of twenty-seven, and about $44,500 was spent in a year for the White House Office. By then, the President received around one hundred letters a day.

When Theodore Roosevelt was President, he had a staff of thirty-eight, and the mail had increased to five hundred letters a day.

When Herbert Hoover was inaugurated in 1929, the President's home and office was a big business that cost $336,280 a year to run. This included the President's salary, $75,000; salaries for the office staff, $96,480; office expenses, $37,800; the President's travel allowance, $25,000; and the cost of keeping up the White House and grounds, $102,000.

However, these were not the only expenses. The Treasury Department paid for the Secret Service men. The White House police force received a separate appropriation; the armed services paid the salaries of the twenty White House aides assigned to the President. All told, there were one hundred and fifty full-time White House employees.

But until Franklin Roosevelt established the Executive Office of the President, no one knew *exactly* how many people worked in the White House. The executive agencies assigned civil servants to the White House as they were needed. Only forty-five to fifty-five persons were paid as White House employees.

Finally President Truman asked the Bureau of the Budget to make a study of everything he did. The Bureau found that in three months, the President

approved 193 executive orders, proclamations, public and private bills;

signed and sent to Congress or government officials 185 messages and letters;

issued 52 press statements;

made 12 speeches;

received 71 government officials;

held 10 cabinet meetings;

held 9 press and radio conferences;

received 321 important visitors;

went to church and other public gatherings 35 times;

went to 3 private luncheons;

was awarded 5 medals.

By 1952, the last year that Truman was in office, the cost of the Presidency had gone up to $3,021,215. Five hundred and two persons worked in the Executive Mansion, the White House Office, and on the White House police staff.

Just think, the first Congress appropriated $640,000 for the operation of the entire Federal Government. Now we need approximately four times that amount just to take care of the White House and the President's Park!

When John Adams entered the White House, 137 people worked for the Federal Government. In 1963, the United States government had almost 5,500,000 civilian employees and members of the armed forces working for it. Because the President is Chief Executive and Commander-in-Chief of the armed forces, all of these people work under his direction through people appointed by him.

Of course, only a few people report to him directly. Of the two hundred and seventy persons who carry the regular office load in the White House, a small number work closely with the President. These are his appointments secretary, his press secretary, his legislative assistant, his personal secretary, and a few others.

Some White House employees may see the President only infrequently, such as the chief of correspondence, who each day measures how many feet of mail the President gets and sees that all the letters are answered, or the chief of the travel service, who coordinates the travel plans of the President, his family, and official household.

Because the President's work load and staff have grown through the years, the amount of office space required has grown too.

In 1909, seven years after the President's offices had been moved into the West Wing, the President's Oval Office was added. At that time the one-story wing also included a Cabinet Room, offices for secretaries, a telegraph and telephone room, a press room, stenographers' rooms, reception rooms, and file rooms.

The wing soon grew crowded, so offices were completed in the East Wing. Before and during World War II, both the East and West Wings were enlarged. Even so, the offices were soon about as crowded as the old offices had been on the Second Floor of the White House. Today some of the people who work in the White House Office actually go to work in the Executive Office Building, which is next door to the White House.

The President does most of his work from his Oval Office in the West Wing. The Office is shaped like the oval rooms in the White House proper, and looks out onto the Rose Garden. Each President furnishes the room to suit his own tastes. President Kennedy had a rocking chair in the room, and used a big carved oak desk which Queen Victoria of Great Britain originally gave to the White House during the administration of President Hayes.

The other important and historic office in the West Wing is the Cabinet Room. It, too, faces the Rose Garden. Separated from the President's Office by the office of his personal secretary, this is the room where the Cabinet meets. The National Security Council meets here too, and the President may see groups in this room when they are too large to meet in his office. A portrait of Thomas Jefferson hangs over the mantel. The table in the center of the room is large and heavy. Around it are black leather armchairs. Each one has the name of a Cabinet member on the back. The President's chair is in the center.

The President's visitors can enter the West Wing through the Northwest Gate entrance, by automobile through the Southwest Gate, or through the West Executive avenue entrance, the basement entrance to the White House offices. Until recently, most of the President's visitors have used the Northwest Gate entrance. Therefore television and movie cameras are usually set up around the entrance, which leads into a large reception room.

The Reception Room is furnished with large comfortable couches, and a huge round table that stands squarely in the middle of the room. The top of the table is usually covered with press cameras. To the right of the Reception Room is the White House Press Room, where the reporters assigned to the White House write and file their stories. To the left is the crowded White House Press Office, where the President's Press Secretary and his staff have their desks. More and more frequently today, the President's visitors enter through the basement, where newsmen are not permitted to take pictures, and go upstairs to the Conference Room. This room, where the President greets his visitors, is also called the Fish Room, because President Franklin Roosevelt placed aquariums and fish tanks here. A huge sailfish caught by President Kennedy in 1953 hung on the wall during his years in office.

One part of the West Wing is called the International Situation area. It contains teletype machines, classified machines from the Central Intelligence Agency and the Department of Defense, a map room, and conference rooms. The machines constantly report the news from foreign countries as well as the United States. The maps show where our military forces are all over the world.

Since the President must be immediately informed of any important world and national development, and because he has the power to make decisions concerning nuclear warfare, he must never be far from a telephone. Even when the President swims in the White House pool, a telephone is only a few feet away. It is always a few feet away, whether he is in a car, asleep, or in a jet.

A telephone is not all that is always close to the President of the United States. The men of the Secret Service are always near the President's side. These men spend every moment trying to prevent just such an event as occurred in Dallas, Texas, on November 22, 1963, when President John F. Kennedy was fatally shot while riding in an open car. When the President goes to church, Secret Service men must inspect the church beforehand. If he visits a doctor, the Secret Service must first examine the office. They are always there.

Before the establishment of the Secret Service, the President was protected by trained bodyguards. Even so, Presidents Lincoln, Garfield, and McKinley were assassinated. After the Secret Service took over, attempts were made to kill Franklin Roosevelt and Harry Truman.

When the President goes somewhere unannounced, on short notice, it is not as difficult to protect him as it is when his plans have been made well known in advance.

As you might expect, the President of the United States is a very busy man. While it is true that he has many people to help him, it is also true that there are many things which only he can do, and many decisions which only he can make, for he has great responsibilities. The way in which each President spends his time varies according to the man. It varies, too, according to the nation's needs, for the President is, above all, in the service of his country and his countrymen. Sometimes the President will have a fairly quiet day. More frequently he is very busy.

On one such busy day, as reported in the August 1964 edition of *American Heritage* magazine, President Johnson arose early and by 7:15 A.M. was reading newspapers and reports. He left the living quarters of the White House at 8:40 for a breakfast with legislative leaders. These breakfasts are usually held weekly.

When President Johnson returned to his office at 9:30, it was humming with activity. He received and placed about twenty-seven telephone calls that day. He gave short speeches to two separate groups in the Rose Garden, and two in his office. He held conferences with the Secretary of the Treasury, with an Assistant Secretary of State, and with a Congressman.

The President had lunch at the Mansion with members of his Cabinet, returning to his office in the late afternoon. He made telephone calls and had conferences with staff members. The Ambassador of Venezuela called at his office.

After more staff meetings, the President signed his mail at about 8:45 P.M. He left his office and returned to the living quarters where he had dinner with Mrs. Johnson about 9:20. After ten o'clock he had a last meeting of the day with the Secretary of Defense.

There is often a gap in President Johnson's schedule between 2:45 and 5:01 P.M. Usually he takes a nap and a swim during this time. This is part of his attempt to take care of himself since his heart attack of 1955.

The President may also have quieter days at the White House, when he sees fewer people and is able to have lunch with his wife and a long swim in the pool. He may spend the evening quietly with Mrs. Johnson and retire early.

Ceremonial Headquarters

BECAUSE the President is the Chief of State of our government, the White House is the ceremonial headquarters of the United States. It is here that the President entertains kings and queens, prime ministers, presidents, or envoys of foreign countries.

He entertains a great many of his own countrymen, too. Some of the people who receive invitations to visit the White House are the top officials of our government. They are justices of the Supreme Court, or members of the President's Cabinet. They are Congressmen or high-ranking officers in the armed forces. Others whom the President invites to the White House aren't connected with the government at all. He invites bankers, industrialists, scientists, labor leaders, artists, and astronauts. He also invites young people and children: foreign students, young musicians and dancers, young men and women who excel in scholarship, or who represent national youth groups such as the 4-H Clubs, the Boy Scouts, or Girl Scouts.

This is the way it has always been. The American Presidents and their wives have always invited many different kinds of people to visit them in the White House. Each year the White House is also visited by nearly two million tourists. They come from every state in the Union and from many foreign countries to see the place where the President lives and works. Today the public rooms in the White House are open to tourists five days a week, from ten in the morning until noon.

Below is the floor plan showing the rooms on the First Floor as they are used today. These rooms are generally included in a public tour of the White House.

The East Room is the first room that the visitor sees on a tour of the White House. This largest room in the White House runs from north to south and is decorated in white and gold. The East Room is the place where invited guests gather before a state occasion, and is also used for plays, concerts, or recitals.

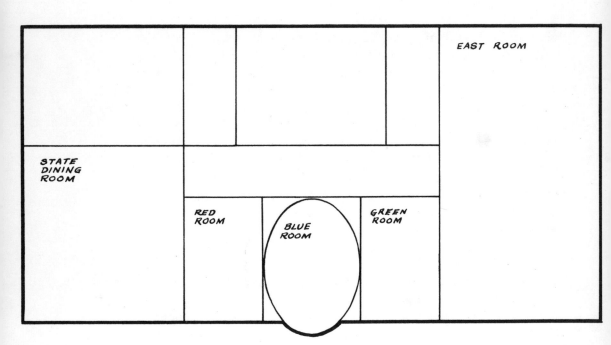

The Green Room is a small parlor frequently used by the President and male guests for after-dinner coffee. It is furnished as John Adams or Thomas Jefferson might have furnished it. After the fire of 1814, it was decorated in green, and it has been called the Green Room ever since.

The Blue Room is one of the three oval-shaped rooms in the White House. It was designed to be the central reception room of the President's House. Redecorated in 1962, the walls are covered with white on white striped satin, and the upholstery and curtains are blue. The main Christmas tree in the White House is sometimes placed in the Blue Room.

The Red Room, frequently used by the First Lady and women guests for after-dinner coffee, is also the scene of small teas and other somewhat informal occasions. The room has fine examples of both French and American craftsmanship. Its scarlet walls hold many Presidential portraits.

Large state dinners are held in the State Dining Room, which seats over one hundred guests. The room was enlarged in 1902 and is decorated in white and gold.

All of these rooms are connected by the Cross Hall. It has marble floors and walls, contains a red carpet, marble busts of Washington and Joel Barlow, an early American patriot, the flag of the United States, and the President's flag.

Visitors are also allowed to see the Library on the Ground Floor, and some groups visit the Diplomatic Reception Room. These rooms are shown in the floor plan on the next page.

The Library was redone in 1962, and it looks like a room of the early 1800's. Its walls are painted pale yellow. The furniture is the work of a famous classical American cabinetmaker named Duncan Phyfe. The books in the room represent American thinking up to the present day.

The Diplomatic Reception Room is an oval room on the Ground Floor. It is used as the entrance to the Mansion by the President and his family, and by guests invited to attend state functions. In 1961,

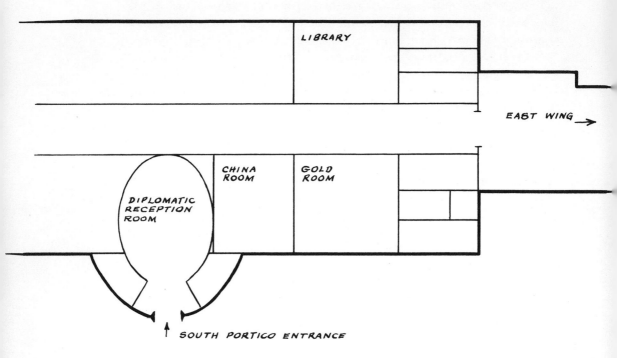

the room was decorated with wallpaper printed in 1834. The paper shows views of five American natural wonders that Europeans have liked: Niagara Falls, the Natural Bridge of Virginia, Boston Harbor, West Point, and New York Bay.

As the ceremonial headquarters of our country, the White House is our national showplace. The official social events which take place there require a great deal of planning. Seating arrangements and rules of etiquette can be very complicated.

The President does not have to worry about these details. A special office in the Department of State, called the Protocol Office, helps the President and First Lady plan for their guests. That is their job. The Protocol Staff knows the customs of all the countries which the guests represent, and helps to make each guest feel comfortable. After all, a diplomat might feel very insulted if he were served food at the White House that his country's religion would not allow him to eat.

When foreign rulers and heads of government visit the United States officially, the Chief of Protocol, who heads the Protocol Office, must arrange to greet the guests. He must see that they meet the President and other important people on time and in the most enjoyable way.

The ways of greeting important visitors from foreign countries have changed through the years. At one time the President would meet foreign leaders in Washington's Union Railroad Station. When Presidents Roosevelt, Truman, and Eisenhower were in office, they usually met their guests at Washington National Airport.

Today a head of state or other important official often sees the President for the first time right on the White House lawn. The guest arrives by helicopter. A red carpet is stretched out across the south lawn. There the President and First Lady await their guests.

Twenty-one cannon shots greet the visiting head of state. The Chief of Protocol meets the visitor at the helicopter, introduces everyone, and the national anthems of the visitor's country and the United States are played.

The dinner parties at which the ruler or president of a foreign country are entertained are very formal affairs.

Hand-engraved invitations are mailed to the guests, requesting their arrival at eight o'clock in the evening. Just before that hour, the guests, in formal evening clothes, begin to arrive at the Southwest Gate. A guard checks their names against the guest list.

In the Diplomatic Reception Room, guests leave their wraps. Upstairs in the North Lobby, each man is given the name of the lady who is to be his dinner partner.

Soon all the one hundred guests are gathered in the East Room. The Marine Band plays "Ruffles and Flourishes," and "Hail to the Chief." The President, First Lady, and guests of honor slowly walk down the grand staircase from the Second Floor through a color guard. They form a receiving line to greet all the guests. Then the President, escorting the wife of the statesman, leads the way to the State Dining Room.

Everything on the long table in the Dining Room is gold and white. The tablecloth is gold and white; the plates are white with gold trim. In the center of the table is a long golden centerpiece brought from France in 1818. The three knives and three forks at each place setting are gold. Even the ashtrays and nut dishes are gold.

Uniformed butlers serve a four-course meal prepared by the French chef. Musicians play softly. If one dinner partner speaks a language which the other cannot understand, an interpreter from the Department of State sits behind them during the meal to translate their conversation.

When everyone has finished dessert, the First Lady rises and leads the ladies into the Red Room. The President leads the gentlemen into the Green Room. After coffee, the party moves back to the East Room. A famous musician may play, or ballet dancers or actors may perform.

At 11 P.M., the guests of honor say good-night to the President and the First Lady. That is the signal for the other guests to leave, too. However, it would not be polite to leave before the guests of honor.

The White House today is a beautiful American home, reflecting the best of our country's early art and design. As home of the President of the United States, center of the workings of this powerful nation, and distinguished showplace for citizen and foreign visitor, the White House is a proud symbol of our national heritage.

The Presidents

GEORGE WASHINGTON	April 30, 1789 – March 3, 1797
JOHN ADAMS	March 4, 1797 – March 3, 1801
THOMAS JEFFERSON	March 4, 1801 – March 3, 1809
JAMES MADISON	March 4, 1809 – March 3, 1817
JAMES MONROE	March 4, 1817 – March 3, 1825
JOHN QUINCY ADAMS	March 4, 1825 – March 3, 1829
ANDREW JACKSON	March 4, 1829 – March 3, 1837
MARTIN VAN BUREN	March 4, 1837 – March 3, 1841
WILLIAM HENRY HARRISON	March 4, 1841 – April 4, 1841
JOHN TYLER	April 6, 1841 – March 3, 1845
JAMES KNOX POLK	March 4, 1845 – March 3, 1849
ZACHARY TAYLOR	March 5, 1849 – July 9, 1850
MILLARD FILLMORE	July 10, 1850 – March 3, 1853
FRANKLIN PIERCE	March 4, 1853 – March 3, 1857
JAMES BUCHANAN	March 4, 1857 – March 3, 1861
ABRAHAM LINCOLN	March 4, 1861 – April 15, 1865
ANDREW JOHNSON	April 15, 1865 – March 3, 1869
ULYSSES S. GRANT	March 4, 1869 – March 3, 1877
RUTHERFORD B. HAYES	March 4, 1877 – March 3, 1881

JAMES A. GARFIELD	March 4, 1881 – September 19, 1881
CHESTER A. ARTHUR	September 20, 1881 – March 3, 1885
GROVER CLEVELAND	March 4, 1885 – March 3, 1889
BENJAMIN HARRISON	March 4, 1889 – March 3, 1893
GROVER CLEVELAND	March 4, 1893 – March 3, 1897
WILLIAM MCKINLEY	March 4, 1897 – September 14, 1901
THEODORE ROOSEVELT	September 14, 1901 – March 3, 1909
WILLIAM HOWARD TAFT	March 4, 1909 – March 3, 1913
WOODROW WILSON	March 4, 1913 – March 3, 1921
WARREN G. HARDING	March 4, 1921 – August 2, 1923
CALVIN COOLIDGE	August 3, 1923 – March 3, 1929
HERBERT C. HOOVER	March 4, 1929 – March 3, 1933
FRANKLIN DELANO ROOSEVELT	March 4, 1933 – April 12, 1945
HARRY S. TRUMAN	April 12, 1945 – January 20, 1953
DWIGHT D. EISENHOWER	January 20, 1953 – January 20, 1961
JOHN F. KENNEDY	January 20, 1961 – November 22, 1963
LYNDON BAINES JOHNSON	November 22, 1963 –

White House Families

JOHN ADAMS:	married Abigail Smith, 1764 children: John Quincy, Thomas, Charles, Abby
THOMAS JEFFERSON:	married Martha Wayles Skelton, 1772 children: Mary, Martha
JAMES MADISON:	married Dorothea Payne Todd, 1794 no children
JAMES MONROE:	married Elizabeth Kortwright, 1786 children: Eliza, Maria
JOHN QUINCY ADAMS:	married Louisa Catherine Johnson, 1797 children: George Washington, John Quincy Jr., Charles Francis, Louisa
ANDREW JACKSON:	married Rachel Donelson Robards, 1791 children: Andrew Jackson Jr. (adopted)
MARTIN VAN BUREN:	married Hannah Hoes, 1807 children: Abraham, John, Martin Jr., Smith Thompson
WILLIAM HENRY HARRISON:	married Anna Symmes, 1795 children: John Scott, William Henry Jr.
JOHN TYLER:	married Letitia Christian, 1813, and Julia Gardiner, 1844 children: Mary, Robert, John, Letitia, Elizabeth, Anne, Alice, Tazewell, David, John, Julia, Lachlan, Lyon, Robert Fitzwalter, Pearl
JAMES KNOX POLK:	married Sarah Childress, 1824 no children

ZACHARY TAYLOR: married Margaret Smith, 1810
children: Sarah Knox, Richard, Elizabeth, Ann

MILLARD FILLMORE: married Abigail Powers, 1826, and Caroline Mc-
Intosh, 1858
children: Mary Abigail, Millard Powers

FRANKLIN PIERCE: married Jane Appleton, 1834
children: Benjamin

JAMES BUCHANAN: bachelor (His niece Harriet Lane served as
hostess)

ABRAHAM LINCOLN: married Mary Todd, 1842
children: Robert, Edward, Willie, Tad

ANDREW JOHNSON: married Eliza McCardle, 1827
children: Martha, Charles, Robert, Mary, Andrew
Jr.

ULYSSES S. GRANT: married Julia B. Dent, 1848
children: Fred, Buck, Jesse, Nellie

RUTHERFORD B. HAYES: married Lucy Ware Webb, 1852
children: Birchard, Webb, Rutherford Jr., Fanny,
Joseph, George, Scott Russell, Manning

JAMES A. GARFIELD: married Lucretia Rudolph, 1858
children: Harry, James, Abram, Irvin, Mollie

CHESTER A. ARTHUR: married Ellen Herndon, 1859
children: Chester Jr., Nellie, William

GROVER CLEVELAND: married Frances Folsom, 1886
children: Ruth, Esther, Marion, Francis, Richard

BENJAMIN HARRISON: married Caroline Scott, 1853, and Mary Scott
Dimmick, 1896
children: Russell, Mary, Elizabeth

WILLIAM MCKINLEY:	married Ida Saxton, 1871 children: Katie, Ida
THEODORE ROOSEVELT:	married Alice Lee, 1880, and Edith Carow, 1886 children: Alice, Theodore Jr., Kermit, Ethel, Archibald, Quentin
WILLIAM HOWARD TAFT:	married Helen Herron, 1886 children: Helen, Robert, Charles
WOODROW WILSON:	married Ellen Axson, 1885, and Edith Galt, 1915 children: Margaret, Eleanor, Jessie
WARREN G. HARDING:	married Florence De Wolfe, 1891 no children
CALVIN COOLIDGE:	married Grace Goodhue, 1905 children: John, Calvin Jr.
HERBERT HOOVER:	married Lou Henry, 1899 children, Herbert Jr., Allan
FRANKLIN DELANO ROOSEVELT:	married Eleanor Roosevelt, 1905 children: Anna, James, Elliott, Franklin Jr., John
HARRY S. TRUMAN:	married Bess Wallace, 1919 children: Margaret
DWIGHT D. EISENHOWER:	married Mamie Geneva Doud, 1916 children: John Sheldon Doud
JOHN F. KENNEDY:	married Jacqueline Lee Bouvier, 1953 children: Caroline, John Jr.
LYNDON BAINES JOHNSON:	married Claudia Taylor, 1934 children: Lynda Bird, Luci Baines

White House "Firsts"

GEORGE WASHINGTON (1789-1797)	the first and only President *not* to live in the White House
JOHN ADAMS (1797-1801)	the first President to live in the White House (1800)
THOMAS JEFFERSON (1801-1809)	the first child born in the White House, the President's grandson (1805)
JAMES MADISON (1809-1817)	the first wedding in the White House, Mrs. Madison's sister (1812)
ANDREW JACKSON (1829-1837)	the first stationary bathtubs installed
WILLIAM HENRY HARRISON (1841-1841)	the first President to die in office, and the first and only President to die in the White House
JOHN TYLER (1841-1845)	the first girl born in the White House, Letitia Christian Tyler (1842)
JAMES K. POLK (1845-1849)	the first gaslights installed in the White House (1848)
FRANKLIN PIERCE (1853-1857)	the first central heating system installed (1853)
RUTHERFORD B. HAYES (1877-1881)	the first time a President's wife was called the "First Lady" (1877)
GROVER CLEVELAND (1885-1889; 1893-1897)	the first and only President to be married in the White House (1886)

BENJAMIN HARRISON (1889-1893)	the first Christmas tree put up in the White House
THEODORE ROOSEVELT (1901-1909)	the first time "The White House" became the official name
WARREN G. HARDING (1921-1923)	the first time a special White House police force was created
CALVIN COOLIDGE (1923-1929)	the first time a full third story was added to the White House, and the first time a radio set was installed
FRANKLIN D. ROOSEVELT (1933-1945)	the first time a swimming pool was built in the White House
HARRY S. TRUMAN (1945-1953)	the first time the White House was completely rebuilt, and the first time a television set was installed

Index

55